Dear v

Thank you for your Purchase!
Enjoy this beautiful Product!

For more Products, please visit us at
papyrumpublishing.com
or
https://www.amazon.com/author/papyrumpublishing

For fun **FREEBIES** please subscribe at
https://www.papyrumpublishing.com/freebies

Stay connected! Please follow us on
Instagram: **@papyrumpublishing**
Facebook: **Papyrum Publishing**

We love your Support and
greatly appreciate your Review on Amazon!!

Wishing you the Best!
Looking forward to seeing you again,
Papyrum Publishing

Have you ever wondered, "**Does God love me?**" Then, you are not the only One! Millions of People in this World ask themselves this Question. It is a great and timeless Question.

Do you want to know the Answer? Then, this Book is right for you!

Let us take a Look into the Bible. So many Chapters in the Bible tell us about God's unsurpassed Love for us. So, what does God love about YOU? This Book is a Collection of **100 Things God loves about You** and Bible Verses proving God's Love for You.

Excited? Then, let's find out!

Let's start out with what the Bible says about Love in General:

Love is patient and is kind; love doesn't envy.
Love doesn't brag, is not proud,
doesn't behave itself inappropriately,
doesn't seek its own way,
is not provoked, takes no account of evil;
doesn't rejoice in unrighteousness,
but rejoices with the truth;
bears all things, believes all things,
hopes all things, endures all things.
Love never fails.
1 Corinthians 13:4-8

You are God's Child.

Behold, how great a love the Father has bestowed on us, that we should be called children of God!

1 John 3:1

You are God's own Creation.

For we are his workmanship, created in Christ Jesus for good works.

Ephesians 2:10

You help Others.

Bear one another's burdens,
and so fulfill the law of Christ.

Galatians 6:2

You are patient.

One who is slow to anger
is better than the mighty.

Proverbs 16:32

Your Notes

You are kind.

And be kind to one another, tenderhearted, forgiving each other, just as God also in Christ forgave you.

Ephesians 4:32

You are humble.

When pride comes, then comes shame, but with humility comes wisdom.

Proverbs 11:2

God loves you.

For God so loved the world, that he gave his one and only Son, that whoever believes in him should not perish, but have eternal life.

John 3:16

Your Faith in him.

God takes pleasure in those who fear him, in those who hope in his loving kindness.

Psalm 147:11

Your Notes

You forgive Others.

For if you forgive [others] their trespasses, your heavenly Father will also forgive you.

Matthew 6:14

Your Love for Others.

A new commandment I give to you, that you love one another, just like I have loved you.

John 13:34

You have Jokes for People around you.

A cheerful heart makes good medicine.

Proverbs 17:22

You understand Others.

Therefore whatever you desire
for [others] to do to you,
you shall also do to them.

Matthew 7:12

Your Notes

You are beautiful.

For I am fearfully
and wonderfully made.

Psalm 139:14

Your Smile.

A glad heart makes a cheerful face.

Proverbs 15:13

Your Friendships.

Perfume and incense bring joy to the
heart; so does earnest counsel
from [one's] friend.

Proverbs 27:9

You encourage People.

Let each one of us please his neighbor
for that which is good,
to be building him up.

Romans 15:2

Your Notes

You have Goals.

The plans of the diligent surely lead to profit.

Proverbs 21:5

You respect your Parents.

Honor your father and your mother, that your days may be long.

Exodus 20:12

You are strong.

Be strong and of good courage.
Don't be afraid, neither be dismayed:
for Yahweh your God is with you.

Joshua 1:9

You are there if someone needs you.

Rejoice with those who rejoice.
Weep with those who weep.

Romans 12:15

Your Notes

You help out those who don't have Much.

He who has pity on the poor lends to God; he will reward him.

Proverbs 19:17

You make Others feel good.

Beloved, let us love one another, for love is of God; and everyone who loves is born of God, and knows God.

1 John 4:7

You take Initiative.

He becomes poor who works with a lazy hand, but the hand of the diligent brings wealth.

Proverbs 10:4

Your inner Beauty.

For God sees not as [a Person] sees; for [a Person] looks at the outward appearance, God looks at the heart.

1 Samuel 16:7

Your Notes

You stay calm.

God will fight for you,
and you shall be still.

Exodus 14:14

You make Others feel important.

You shall love your neighbor
as yourself.

Mark 12:31

You know what People around you need.

Each of you not just looking to his own things, but each of you also to the things of others.

Philippians 2:4

You spend Time with Others.

Not forsaking our own assembling together.

Hebrews 10:25

Your Notes

You lift up Others when they fall.

For if they fall, the one will lift up his fellow; but woe to him who is alone when he falls.

Ecclesiastes 4:10

You don't judge People.

Don't judge, so that you won't be judged.

Matthew 7:1

Your Prayers to God.

Pray without ceasing.

1 Thessalonians 5:17

You think your Decisions through.

But you remain in the things
which you have learned
and have been assured of.

2 Timothy 3:14

Your Notes

You believe in Jesus Christ.

Believe in the Lord Jesus Christ,
and you will be saved,
you and your household.

Acts 16:31

You stick with Others even in bad Times.

But there is a friend
who sticks closer than a brother.

Proverbs 18:24

The Food you make.

Give us today our daily bread.

Matthew 6:11

You accept Others as they are.

Therefore accept one another, even as Christ also accepted you.

Romans 15:7

Your Notes

You take Things easy.

For everything there is a season, and a time for every purpose under heaven.

Ecclesiastes 3:1

You are generous.

Remember this: he who sows sparingly will also reap sparingly. He who sows bountifully will also reap bountifully.

2 Corinthians 9:6

You search for God's Message.

Open my eyes, that I may see wondrous things out of your law.

Ecclesiastes 3:1

You have a big Heart.

That in the good ground, these are such as in an honest and good heart.

Luke 8:15

Your Notes

You always trust in God.

Trust in God with all your heart,
don't lean on your own understanding.

Proverbs 3:5

You don't give up.

But you be strong,
and don't let your hands be slack;
for your work shall be rewarded.

2 Chronicles 15:7

You work toward your Goals.

Forgetting the things which are behind, and stretching forward to the things which are before.

Philippians 3:13

You care for Others when they are sick.

If I then, the Lord and the Teacher, have washed your feet, you also ought to wash one another's feet.

John 13:14

Your Notes

You are grateful.

Continue steadfastly in prayer,
watching therein with thanksgiving.

Colossians 4:2

You are genuine.

Let love be without hypocrisy.
Abhor that which is evil.
Cling to that which is good.

Romans 12:9

You are patient.

He who is slow to anger
has great understanding.

Proverbs 14:29

Your hard Work.

And whatever you do, work heartily.

Colossians 3:23

Your Notes

Your Courage.

Be strong and of good courage,
don't be afraid, nor be scared of them:
for Yahweh your God,
he it is who does go with you.

Deuteronomy 31:6

You make Time
for Others.

Give to him who asks you,
and don't turn away him
who desires to borrow from you.

Matthew 5:42

Your Commitment.

No one, having put his hand to the plow, and looking back, is fit for the Kingdom of God.

Luke 9:62

You are wise.

Therefore watch carefully how you walk, not as unwise, but as wise.

Ephesians 5:15

Your Notes

You are not wasteful.

Gather up the broken pieces which are left over, that nothing be lost.

John 6:12

You read the Scripture.

Every Scripture is God-breathed and profitable for teaching, for reproof, for correction, and for instruction in righteousness.

2 Timothy 3:16

You comfort People when they feel sad.

We may be able to comfort those who are in any affliction.

2 Corinthians 1:4

You Keep Others' Secrets to yourself.

But one who is of a trustworthy spirit is one who keeps a secret.

Proverbs 11:13

Your Notes

You keep your Word.

I will not break my covenant,
nor alter what my lips have uttered.

Psalm 89:34

You take care of yourself.

Or don't you know that your body
is a temple of the Holy Spirit which
is in you, which you have from God?

1 Corinthians 6:19

You respect Animals.

For every animal of the forest is mine,
and the livestock on a thousand hills.
I know all the birds of the mountains.
The wild animals of the field are mine.

Psalm 50:10-11

You respect Others around you.

Therefore whatever you desire for men
to do to you, you shall also do to them;
for this is the law and the prophets.

Matthew 7:12

Your Notes

You give 2nd Chances.

Jesus said, "Father, forgive them, for they don't know what they are doing."

Luke 23:34

You check on Others.

Most certainly I tell you, inasmuch as you did it to one of the least of these my brothers, you did it to me.

Matthew 25:40

You encourage People.

Let no corrupt speech proceed out of your mouth, but such as is good for building up as the need may be, that it may give grace to those who hear.

Ephesians 4:29

You like to share.

But don't forget to be doing good and sharing, for with such sacrifices God is well pleased.

Hebrews 13:16

Your Notes

You stand up for Others.

Open your mouth, judge righteously,
and serve justice
to the poor and needy.

Proverbs 31:9

You don't expect anything in Return.

Do good, and lend, expecting nothing
back; and your reward will be great.

Luke 6:35

You give Importance to healthy Food.

It is not good to eat much honey.

Proverbs 25:27

You also appreciate the little Things in Life.

He who is faithful in a very little is faithful also in much.

Luke 16:10

Your Notes

You enjoy the Nature.

In his hand are the deep places of the earth. The heights of the mountains are also his. The sea is his[...]. His hands formed the dry land.

Psalm 95:4-5

You make Plans.

For which of you, desiring to build a tower, doesn't first sit down and count the cost, to see if he has enough to complete it?

Luke 14:28

Your singing.

I will incline my ear to a proverb.
I will open my riddle on the harp.

Psalm 49:4

You are peaceful.

In peace I will both lay myself down
and sleep, for you, God alone,
make me live in safety.

Psalm 4:8

Your Notes

You are a great Christian.

If anyone desires to come after me,
let him deny himself, and
take up his cross, and follow me.

Matthew 16:24

You support Others.

Bear one another's burdens,
and so fulfill the law of Christ.

Galatians 6:2

You don't punish.

Don't seek revenge yourselves, beloved, but give place to God's wrath. For it is written, "Vengeance belongs to me; I will repay, says the Lord.

Romans 12:19

You choose your friends carefully.

A righteous person is cautious in friendship.

Proverbs 12:26

Your Notes

You are gentle.

Let your gentleness be known to all.
The Lord is at hand.

Philippians 4:5

You are not jealous.

For where jealousy and
selfish ambition are,
there is confusion and every evil deed.

James 3:16

You learn from your Mistakes.

For a righteous [one] falls seven times, and rises up again.

Proverbs 24:16

You are fair.

Blessed are those who keep justice.

Psalm 106:3

Your Notes

You spend wisely.

There is precious treasure and oil
in the dwelling of the wise;
but a foolish [one] swallows it up.

Proverbs 21:20

You make a Difference
wherever you can.

Let him know that he who turns
a sinner from the error of his way
will save a soul from death.

James 5:20

You make Others happy.

You have put gladness in my heart,
more than when their grain
and their new wine are increased.

Psalm 4:7

You treat people equal.

There is neither Jew nor Greek,
there is neither slave nor free man,
there is neither male nor female;
for you are all one in Christ Jesus.

Galatians 3:28

Your Notes

You say: "Everything will be OK".

Casting all your worries on him, because he cares for you.

1 Peter 5:7

You don't brag.

Thus says God, Don't let the wise man glory in his wisdom, neither let the mighty man glory in his might, don't let the rich man glory in his riches.

Jeremiah 9:23

You share God's Message.

He said to them, "Go into all the world, and preach the Good News to the whole creation.

Mark 16:15

You are content.

Not that I speak in respect to lack, for I have learned in whatever state I am, to be content in it.

Philippians 4:11

Your Notes

You attend Church.

For where two or three
are gathered together in my name,
there I am in the midst of them.

Matthew 18:20

You are not distracted by worldly Things.

Denying ungodliness and worldly
lusts, we would live soberly, righteously,
and godly in this present world.

Titus 2:12

You avoid bad Influence.

Blessed is the man who doesn't walk in the counsel of the wicked, nor stand in the way of sinners.

Psalm 1:1

You respect the Elderly.

You shall rise up before the gray head, and honor the face of an old man, and you shall fear your God.

Leviticus 19:32

Your Notes

You have a
Heart for Children.

Allow the little children [...] come to me; for the Kingdom of Heaven belongs to ones like these.

Matthew 19:14

You are not selfish.

Each of you not just looking to his own things, but each of you also to the things of others.

Philippians 2:4

You make Time for God.

But seek first God's Kingdom, and his righteousness; and all these things will be given to you as well.

Matthew 6:33

You watch your Words.

He who would love life,
and see good days,
let him keep his tongue from evil,
and his lips from speaking deceit.

1 Peter 3:10

Your Notes

You obey God's Rules.

Show me your ways, God.
Teach me your paths.

Psalm 25:4

You have Discipline.

He is in the way of life who heeds
correction, but he who forsakes reproof
leads others astray.

Proverbs 10:17

Your Imperfections.

If we confess our sins, he is faithful
and righteous to forgive us the sins,
and to cleanse us from
all unrighteousness.

1 John 1:9

Your Talents.

Every good gift and every perfect gift
is from above, coming down from the
Father of lights, with whom can be
no variation, nor turning shadow.

James 1:17

Your Notes

Made in United States
Troutdale, OR
08/21/2024

22224033R00044